Stuff Every

VEGETARIAN

Should Know

By Katherine McGuire

Copyright © 2017 by Quirk Productions, Inc.

Library of Congress Cataloging in Publication Number: 2016960821

ISBN: 978-1-68369-005-4

Printed in China
Typeset in Goudy, Requiem, and Trade Gothic

Designed by Molly Rose Murphy
Production management by John J. McGurk

Quirk Books
215 Church Street
Philadelphia, PA 19106
quirkbooks.com

10 9 8 7 6 5 4 3 2 1

Stuff Every

VEGETARIAN

Should Know

By Katherine McGuire

QUIRK BOOKS
PHILADELPHIA

For the animals—human
and nonhuman alike

INTRODUCTION 8

GETTING STARTED

Veggie Vocabulary 12

Reasons to Feel Awesome 18

NUTRITION

Protein 101 26

Complete Proteins Cheat Sheet 28

16 Global Complete Protein Combos 30

Essential Nutrients 32

Vegetarian Food Pyramid 37

Vegetarianism and Special Dietary Needs . . . 38

PREPPING YOUR KITCHEN

How to Stock Your Shelves 44

Emphasizing Veggies 48

Where to Shop 52

Secrets of the Bulk Bin 54

How to Cook Dried Beans 56

How to Cook Grains 59

A Note on Cooking Bulgur and Couscous . . . 62

A Trick for Cooking White Rice 64

Where to Save and Where to Splurge 66

COOKING

How to Read Recipes 70

How to Make Recipes Vegetarian 73

How to Substitute Ingredients. 76

7 Basic Flavor Combos. 81

Sample 7-Day Menu 83

Hearty Breakfasts and Brunches 91

Inspired Sandwich Lunches. 93

Bag Snacks 95

Flavor Bases 98

How to Make an Awesome Bean Soup 100

How to Make Amazing Stir-Fry. 103

How to Make Tofu Delicious 106

5 Great Bacon Substitutes 109

Umami Hacks. 112

How Not to Be Hungry 24/7 114

LIVING THE VEGETARIAN LIFE

Handling Tough Situations with Grace 118

4 Little White Lies 123

Dining Out as a Vegetarian 124

Traveling as a Vegetarian 129

5 Stealthy Nonvegetarian Foods 132

Acquired Tastes
   (and How to Acquire Them) 134

RESOURCES 137
ACKNOWLEDGMENTS 144
RESOURCES 137
ACKNOWLEDGMENTS 144

Introduction

Congratulations! You've decided to eat less meat. Whether you're motivated by health, animal welfare, or environmental, social, or religious reasons, you're in good company. There are hundreds of millions of happy vegetarians around the world. Welcome to the veg club!

Even though you're in good company, you might feel a little overwhelmed. It's hard at first to know how to cook, what to buy, or how to make your way through a culture that doesn't always make your new dietary choice easy. For all those millions of vegetarians, you're still outnumbered: more people eat meat than don't.

But you're going to gain a *lot* more than you're giving up: peace of mind, new food options, health benefits, and much more. Great stuff is in store for you when you put plants on your plate.

This handy-dandy vegetarian primer will teach you how to stock your pantry, cook a few basics, and navigate social situations as a vegetarian in a meat-eating world. You'll learn how to stay full and satisfy cravings. You'll fall in love with unfamiliar ingredients and spices, you'll take care of your health, and you'll find a lot of satisfaction in living well and with compassion. Don't worry so much about "doing it right" at this point. Just focus on making good choices for yourself and your body. And trust me when I say that you'll have fun in the process.

Let's get this vegetarian adventure started!

Getting

STARTED

Veggie Vocabulary

If you're new to vegetarianism, chances are you're learning about unfamiliar dishes, ingredients, and other lingo. Or you've heard these words, but you're not sure what they mean. Here are some common vegetarian terms demystified.

Carnism: A term used first by social psychologist Melanie Joy, who wrote that attitudes about meat reflect unconscious social prejudice. The website Carnism.org defines it as "the invisible belief system, or ideology, that conditions people to eat certain animals. . . . Because carnism is invisible, people rarely realize that eating animals is a choice, rather than a given."

Flexitarian: A person who tries to eat vegetarian most of the time, but is *flexible*. This person is usually trying to reduce, but not eliminate, their meat consumption.

Freegan: Someone who won't pay money for or otherwise financially incentivize the production of animal products, but will eat non-veg foods otherwise destined for the garbage stream. Typically, this is someone who foregrounds ecological concerns and strives for a low-waste lifestyle.

Lacto-ovo vegetarian: A person who eats dairy ("lacto"), eggs ("ovo"), and plants ("vege") but not animals.

Meatless Mondays: A global movement to reduce meat consumption by eating veg on Mondays. Many restaurants now offer Meatless Monday specials. Participating in this weekly practice is a great way to try delicious veggie dishes if you're not ready to take the full plunge.

Miso: A sweet, tangy, salty, and savory fermented soybean paste. In Japan, its many varieties are appreciated like fine cheeses. Traditionally used as a soup base, it's also great in sauces, marinades, and spreads.

Nutritional yeast: Savory, nutty, cheesy-tasting yellow flakes that you can find in the bulk aisle of natural foods stores. Some people call it "nooch." Enjoy it sprinkled onto popcorn or stirred into creamy sauces for a flavor and protein boost.

Omnivore: Someone who does not observe dietary restrictions (i.e., eats animals as well as plants). Biologically, all humans are omnivores because we're physiologically able to obtain nutrition from animal and plant sources. Here, though, we're talking about *choice* of food.

Pescatarian: Someone who does not eat land animals but consumes aquatic animals, like fish and shellfish.

Pulses: An umbrella term for a part of the legume family that includes beans, lentils, and peas. These terms refer to green peas, chickpeas, lentils . . . basically everything beanlike except for soybeans, which have a much higher fat content, and groundnuts (for example, peanuts).

Raw: In the context of food choices, this refers to eating only uncooked and minimally processed foods, typically for health reasons. People who eat this way aren't necessarily vegetarians, and many consider it a fad diet. But raw restaurants usually serve lots of veg options.

Quinoa: Pronounced "KEEN-wah." A nutritious, light, and fluffy seed, originally from Peru, that cooks up like a grain. It is delicious in pilafs.

Seitan: Some people call this "wheat meat." It is the protein that holds bread dough together (aka gluten) that has been kneaded to knit the molecules together and has had the starch all washed out. As a beef stand-in, it's savory, toothsome, and chewy—and delicious grilled, roasted, or even deep-fried.

Speciesism: An unconscious prejudice toward the rights of a particular species, most often humans, dogs, and cats. Because of this bias, we tend to think that certain animals should be protected from harms that are commonly inflicted on others. Horrified by the Yulin Dog Meat Festival but not by the thought of factory-farmed pigs being trucked to a slaughterhouse? This is speciesism at work.

Tempeh: A nutty-tasting, high-protein cultured soybean cake, pronounced "TEM-pay." Invented in Indonesia, it stars in regional dishes like *gado-gado*, *pecel*, or *tahu tempe* (look online for recipes) and is equally good panfried and served on a bun veggie-burger-style. You can also fry it in thin strips as "bacon."

Tofu: The solidified curds from soy milk. You've probably encountered tofu before, but many varieties exist: water-packed and firm, silken, dried, in puffs, pressed, shredded, and more. East Asian grocers tend to offer a wide range of styles.

VB6: An acronym for "vegan before six," describing a diet in which breakfast and lunch are vegan, but anything goes at dinner. A variant is 5:2 vegetarianism, in which a person eats veg five days a week and then eats meat on weekends.

Veg*n: A catchall term when referring to vegans and vegetarians together. Derived from the use of the asterisk as a wildcard operator in computer searches.

Veganism: A lifestyle that attempts to eliminate the use of all animal-derived products, in one's diet and beyond. That means no meat, fish, milk, eggs, honey, wool, leather, musk, tallow, lanolin, animal-tested cosmetics, trips to amusement

parks where confined animals are used as enter-
tainment, etc.

Vegetarian: A person who does not eat animals—
no cows, goats, pigs, chickens, ducks, dogs, fish,
humans, or anything else. Motivations range from
environmentalism to personal health to concern
for animal welfare to religion.

Yuba: Also called tofu skin or bean curd sheet.
These protein-dense, crispy dried sheets are made
from the layer that forms on top of soy milk as
it is being boiled. Rehydrate them in water for a
chewy, savory ingredient that you can form into
rolls and fry or braise.

. . . And One Thing to Look Out For

Gluten free: Foods that are "gluten free" have
nothing to do with vegetarianism. But sometimes when you ask for a vegetarian menu, you'll
find that waitstaff may tell you about gluten-free
options instead. Be prepared for this. Just gently
remind them of what you do and don't eat.

Reasons to Feel Awesome

Just by skipping the meat and eating something equally delicious, you're saving lives, water, greenhouse gas emissions, and your cardiovascular system. And by the end of this book, I hope you'll find that you're getting back more than you're giving up—new dining options, favorite foods you haven't tried yet, and maybe even a sense of community! The following facts and figures should help.

Awesome Stuff You're Doing for Animals

If you're a vegetarian living in the United States, how many lives are you saving? Calculations vary but run anywhere between 100 and 500 animals a year. According to data scientist Harish Sethu, bearing in mind both the animals killed for eating and the "collateral damage" of animals killed during grain farming or fishing, one person's choice to go veg saves more than an animal a day—over 350 animals a year, of which at least 25 will be land animals such as cows, pigs, goats, and chickens.

Here's what you're opting out of: Per USDA statistics, nearly 9 *billion* chickens were sent to USDA-overseen slaughter in 2015. With 320 million people in the U.S., that's more than 25 chickens per person per year. The figures for other animals: almost 29 million cows, 450 thousand calves, 115 million pigs, 2 million sheep and lambs, 230 million turkeys, and 28 million ducks.

If you stop eating meat at age 20 and keep at it, by the time you retire you'll have saved at least 1,000 land animal lives.

Awesome Stuff You're Doing for Your Health

Going veg is obviously great for animals, but it's pretty awesome for your health, too.

- **Your life expectancy could be longer.** Many studies show an association between plant-based eating and reduced mortality rates, particularly in deaths caused by cardiac and colorectal problems. In the United Kingdom and Australia, some life insurance companies even offer reduced rates for vegetarians.

- **You're taking care of your heart.** There's no cholesterol in anything plant-derived, and as a vegetarian, more of your diet is likely to come from plants. In fact, meat consumption is correlated with higher rates of heart disease. Your arteries will thank you!

- **You get the benefits of beans.** If you're going veg, you're almost surely going to eat more beans, which provide protein, soluble dietary fiber, and a dose of iron that's comparable gram-for-gram to a steak.

- **You can "eat the rainbow."** This is a trendy way of saying that you're piling your plate with fruits and veggies in all sorts of colors every day. A wide range of color gives you an equally wide range of beneficial nutrients, micronutrients, and only-in-plants phytochemicals like beta-carotene and lycopene.

- **You're tuned in.** Bringing your attention to what's on your plate and how it makes your body feel can benefit physical and mental well-being alike. Pop psychologists call it "mindful eating." Rock those deliberate choices!

- **You're kicking the nasties out.** Pollutants accumulate in higher concentrations the farther up the food chain you go. Fish are full of mercury. The World Health Organization labels processed meat as carcinogenic and red meat as probably carcinogenic. By eating veg, you're skipping all of that.

- **You can feel good about yourself.** Don't underestimate the psychological benefit and peace of mind of a cruelty-free diet. Take a minute to bask in your smug, self-righteous glow. I won't tell anyone!

Awesome Stuff
You're Doing for the Environment

A recent study from the University of Oxford showed that a transition to plant-based diets globally could reduce agriculture-related greenhouse gas emissions anywhere from 29 to 70 percent by 2050. Further research out of the University of Chicago shows that if the U.S. reduced meat consumption by only 20 percent, the environmental effect would be equivalent to everyone in the U.S. switching to driving a Prius.

The Vegan Calculator estimates that every day, in addition to an average of one animal life, a vegan saves:

- 20 pounds of CO_2 emissions
- 30 square feet of forest
- 40 pounds of grain
- 1,100 gallons of water

Awesome Things You're Doing Financially

- **You're skipping on subsidies.** In the U.S., tax dollars pay for meat through USDA subsidies at the cost of millions of dollars annually to large-scale animal agriculture, keeping it artificially cheap. Don't offload your diet onto taxpayers!

- **You're saving on doctor's visits.** If you pay attention to nutrition, load your diet with minimally processed fruits, veggies, and legumes, and cut out the high-cholesterol, carcinogenic stuff, you're doing your health savings account a favor.

- **Your wallet thanks you.** A pound of lentils costs $1.50. A pound of beef costs four bucks. Enough said. Put the rest in your savings account . . . or splurge on truffle oil and mock bacon.

NUTRITION

Protein 101

One of the most common questions vegetarians are asked is, "But where do you get your protein?" To answer it, and to ensure you fuel yourself well, let's take a crash course in biochemistry.

You get calories (meaning energy—a calorie is a unit of energy) from three types of food sources, called **macronutrients**:

- carbohydrates (4 calories per gram)
- protein (4 calories per gram)
- fat (9 calories per gram)

Aim to consume the same amount of energy your body needs to get through the day—too many calories means weight gain, and too little means weight loss. For most people, that amount of energy equates to 2,000 calories or so, though your needs depend on your age, sex, and physical activity level.

Most foods contain a mix of the three macronutrients, in addition to the vitamins, minerals, omega fatty acids, and phytochemicals classified as **micronutrients**. A well-rounded diet includes all these substances, though when you go vegetarian, the one people fret about most is protein. Try to get about 1 gram of protein a day for every 2 pounds of your body weight (or more if you're pregnant or an athlete; check with a health professional, and see page 38).

Protein is the building block of almost all tissues in the body, especially muscle tissue. It is made of smaller building blocks called **amino acids**. About twenty amino acids are necessary for building body tissues, but your body can make only about half of those on its own. That means you need to get the rest from your diet. If you can get all the right stuff within a 24-hour period, you've got yourself a **complete protein**: everything your body needs to synthesize the tissues that make up your body. Amazing that your body is a state-of-the-art protein-manufacturing machine, right?

Soy foods and quinoa are complete proteins. Vegetarians can also get complete proteins by pairing two different foods that have some but not all of the amino acids. Grains and legumes, for example, fill in each other's amino acid gaps. Cover your bases by eating them within the same day.

Complete Proteins Cheat Sheet

COLUMN A: GRAINS	
Wheat	bread, pasta, cereal, wheat berries, doughnuts
Oats	whole oats, oatmeal, granola, oatcakes
Rice	white rice, brown rice, black rice, rice cakes, pilafs, rice flour treats, mochi puffs, congee
Millet	on its own, mixed in a salad, as a pilaf mixed 50/50 with quinoa, baked into a dense bread
Corn	on the cob, as *masa* or in *arepas*, hominy, tortillas, corn bread, polenta, Doritos, Corn Nuts
Other grains	teff (the basis for Ethiopian injera bread), amaranth, buckwheat, Kamut, and more

Pair any of the items in column A with one
from column B to form a complete protein.

COLUMN B: BEANS/LEGUMES/PULSES	
Beans	kidney beans, chickpeas, mung beans, black-eyed peas, cannellini beans, black beans, refried beans, baked beans, falafel
Peas	yellow peas, green peas, fresh peas, canned peas, pea soup, wasabi pea snacks
Lentils	brown lentils, red lentils, fancy French lentils, lentil crisps, *poppadum*, dal, *rasam*, *misir wot*
Nuts and seeds	peanuts, almonds, cashews, hazelnuts, chestnuts, sunflower seeds, sesame seeds, nut butters and tahini

16 Global Complete Protein Combos

To recap: your amazing body can build a complete protein from amino acids that you eat within 24 hours of one another . . . but why wait longer than a single meal? Many world cultures have been making delicious, meat-free complete protein meals for thousands of years, and the internet is full of good recipes riffing on these combinations.

1. Indian dal and basmati rice

2. Japanese *natto* (fermented soybeans) and short-grain rice

3. Chinese kung pao tofu

4. Indonesian *sambal goreng tempeh* (panfried soybean cake with chili-shallot sauce)

5. Arabic *mojadarah* (lentils and caramelized onions with rice or bulgur wheat)

6. East African injera and *shiro* (teff bread and chickpea stew)

7. Central Asian *pullao* (rice pilaf) with walnuts or pistachios

8. Italian cannellini bean, rice, and escarole soup

9. Polish pea soup with rye bread

10. Middle Eastern hummus and pita

11. Rice and mung bean congee (Chinese savory rice porridge), or sweet and coconutty *payar kanji* (Indian rice porridge)

12. Central American tostadas with refried pinto beans

13. Caribbean black bean soup with rice

14. Vietnamese seitan braised in soy-sauce broth

15. Moroccan couscous with chickpeas

16. West African *maafe* (peanut and veggie stew) with millet

Essential Nutrients

Has Aunt Roberta been hounding you about your protein intake ever since you stopped eating her pork chops? Never fear! With a little planning and common sense, you can get all the vitamins and minerals you need to stay healthy on a veg diet. Keep an eye out for these nutrients:

CALCIUM

Calcium builds bones and helps your nervous system. The FDA recommends that teens get 1,300 milligrams, adults get 1,000 milligrams, and women over 50 get 1,200 milligrams per day. Although people commonly think of dairy first, black-eyed peas, broccoli, dark leafy greens, sesame seeds and tahini, fortified plant milks, and fortified orange juice are also rich sources of calcium. Also watch your vitamin D and magnesium intake to enhance absorption.

UNREFINED FATS

Unrefined fats, such as those from avocados, canola oil, olive oil, or nuts, are your friend, so don't be shy. These unsaturated fats, consumed in moderation, will help control cholesterol levels and keep you full between meals, too.

IRON

Iron helps blood cells carry oxygen for energy, prevents anemia, and is important for healthy growth and development. If you menstruate, the FDA recommends that you get 18 milligrams per day, and if you don't menstruate, 8 milligrams. Beans and dark leafy greens are highly bioavailable sources (meaning the iron in them is easily absorbed by the body). So are blackstrap molasses, cocoa powder, prunes, raisins, cashews, sunflower seeds, and pumpkin seeds. Eating these foods with something high in vitamin C—like a squeeze of citrus or a dollop of tomato sauce—enhances absorption.

OMEGA-3 FATTY ACIDS

These are important for cardiovascular and nervous system health. Ground flaxseeds, flax oil, chia seeds, canola oil, some soy products, hemp seeds, and walnuts are good sources of the omega-3 fatty acid alpha-linolenic acid (ALA). Consume a little bit daily—5 walnut halves, 2 teaspoons of hemp oil or chia seeds, or 1 teaspoon of flax oil is enough. Vegetarians tend to be low on the other long-chain omega-3s, docosahexaenoic acid (DHA) and eicosapentaenoic acid (EPA), so take a DHA-EPA supplement derived from algae.

PROTEIN

Protein is found in every tissue in your body, helps with growth and repair, and is important for muscle strength. The FDA recommends that an adult on a 2,000-calorie diet consume 50 grams per day. Protein is commonly associated with meat and eggs, but elephants, gorillas, and racehorses get their protein from plants, and so can you! See "Protein 101" (page 26) for more information.

VITAMIN B$_{12}$

Vitamin B$_{12}$ helps you form neurons and red blood cells, which are important. You absolutely cannot get this vitamin from plant foods, and you can do permanent damage before you notice deficiency symptoms like depression or anemia, so don't mess around here. Happily, the supplement is cheap and widely available. The NIH recommends that the average adult get 2.4 micrograms per day, but because of the low risk of overdose, try a daily 500-microgram oral supplement.

VITAMIN D

Vitamin D helps the body absorb calcium. Try to get 600 iu (that's international units) a day. If you spend time in the sunshine every day, your body will make a certain amount, but mushrooms, fortified juices and plant milks, and supplements are also good sources. If you're vegan and buying a supplement, note that D_2 is typically plant-derived, but D_3 supplements are usually derived from lanolin, a by-product of industrial sheep farming.

Some general tips for a well-rounded diet:

- Focus on unprocessed foods, get enough protein, and eat a wide variety of beans, grains, and vegetables, not the same thing every day.

- Ask a dietitian or a doctor with nutrition education for advice.

- Pay attention to your body and what makes you feel good to eat—not just while you're eating it, but in the two or three hours *after* you eat it.

- If you're craving kale, eat kale. If you're craving hummus, eat hummus. If you're craving chocolate, maybe don't eat an entire chocolate cake—but satisfy your craving, such as with a square of dark chocolate, and savor it. In other words, treat yourself kindly!

Vegetarian Food Pyramid

Similar to the USDA food groups guide, this pyramid shows the basic components of a well-rounded vegetarian diet.

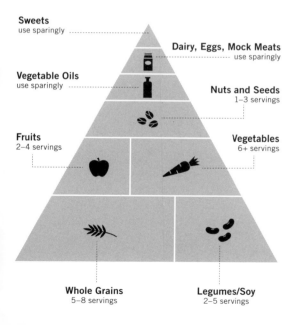

Sweets
use sparingly

Dairy, Eggs, Mock Meats
use sparingly

Vegetable Oils
use sparingly

Nuts and Seeds
1–3 servings

Fruits
2–4 servings

Vegetables
6+ servings

Whole Grains
5–8 servings

Legumes/Soy
2–5 servings

Vegetarianism and Special Dietary Needs

Concerned about how your vegetarian diet might impact your health or lifestyle? Worry not! Many vegetarians before you have maintained their diet and succeeded in these circumstances. If any of these special concerns apply to you, consulting a medical professional is advised.

PREGNANCY AND BREASTFEEDING

According to registered dietitian Virginia Messina, author of *Vegan for Her*, you will need 15 to 20 percent more calories when pregnant and breastfeeding than before you were pregnant. In addition, you will need up to 50 percent more of certain nutrients, particularly protein, folic acid, other B vitamins, iodine, iron, and zinc. When breastfeeding, be sure to get enough vitamin A, vitamin C, vitamin D, vitamin B_{12}, and omega-3s.

ATHLETES

The most important thing: Make sure you get enough calories! Balance the energy (i.e., calories) you burn with the amount you take in. Be sure you're eating plenty of protein, which helps build muscle, and lots of high-iron foods to help your blood carry oxygen, like beans and leafy greens. Look to resources like the *No Meat Athlete* blog, VRG.org's section on athletes, and books by vegan or vegetarian endurance athletes, including Scott Jurek and Brendan Brazier.

TEENS

Teenagers may need more calories than adults. In terms of nutrition, focus on protein, iron, calcium, vitamin B_{12}, vitamin D, and zinc. See the Teen Vegetarian resources on EatRight.org.

PARENTS

Raising your child vegetarian? Find a well-informed and supportive pediatrician. Combine an online search for a vegetarian-friendly doctor with a close look at their credentials—in the U.S., you want someone with an MD or DO degree.

Your child is their own person; let them make their own choices outside the house. Feel free to share with them why you've made dietary choices within your family, but show them that you trust their ability to make their own decisions. If they ask, teach them about vegetarian cooking and meal planning.

SENIORS

As you age, calorie needs decrease, and nutrient absorption may become more difficult. Emphasize nutrient-dense foods, and ask your doctor if supplements are necessary. Make sure you get enough calcium to prevent the progression of osteoporosis. Almonds, tahini, soybeans, dried figs, broccoli, kale, bok choy, and milk (either dairy or calcium-fortified plant derived) are all good options.

PETS

Think carefully! You chose to go veg based on your values, thought process, and what feels good for your body . . . and probably out of respect for animals. The nonhuman animals you live with don't have the choices you do. Make sure you show them respect the way you're trying to show respect to farmed animals. Know the difference between an obligate carnivore and other animals.

- Cats are obligate carnivores. They *cannot* eat a vegetarian diet and be healthy.

- Dogs, like humans, can eat an entirely vegetarian diet and still be well, but only if their diet is carefully planned. Talk to a trusted veterinarian if you want to go this route.

Prepping Your

KITCHEN

How to Stock Your Shelves

Keeping your pantry, freezer, and fridge well stocked and organized will make for more efficient weeknight meals and easier grocery shopping. Remember: what goes in your grocery cart is what goes into your body, so shop with intention and make a list ahead of time.

Dried Pantry Foods

- 2–3 varieties of beans
- 2–3 varieties of whole grains
- 2–3 types of nuts (or seeds, if you're allergic) for garnishes and snacking
- Nut butter (or nut-less butter such as sunflower seed butter)
- Tahini (roasted is tastier than raw)
- Soy sauce or tamari
- 2–3 boxes of dried pasta in different shapes
- Flours for baking

- Sugar and/or other sweeteners
- Canned tomatoes (crushed, chunks, and paste)
- Canned coconut milk for curries and the occasional super-indulgent creamy smoothie/milkshake
- Cartons of nondairy milk if you prefer it over dairy
- Vegetable broth
- Umami flavors
  - sun-dried tomatoes
  - dried mushrooms
  - nutritional yeast
  - Chinese dried black beans
- Smoky flavors
  - chipotle peppers (ground, dried, or canned in adobo sauce)
  - liquid smoke
  - smoked paprika
- Asian condiments and flavor pastes (Thai red curry paste, *sambal oelek*, sriracha, chili bean paste, hoisin sauce)

- Salsa and hot sauce
- 2 or 3 oils: cooking-grade olive oil and a neutral-flavored oil like canola or vegetable oil, plus nice oils for making salad dressings or finishing stir-fries
- 2 or 3 vinegars such as red wine, apple cider, rice, black (for Chinese food), and balsamic (for Italian food)
- Spices that go with your favorite cuisines (start with a few dried herbs and spices and build from there)
- A few treats and snacks: tortilla chips, crackers, rice cakes, chocolate chips, granola bars, cookies, wasabi peas, popcorn, etc.

Fridge/Bread Box

- A few fresh fruits and veggies
- Bread
- Free-range eggs (if you eat them)
- Fresh tofu (if you have plans to cook it)
- Miso paste for soups, sauces, and dressings
- Dairy milk (if you drink it)

Freezer

- Firm tofu sliced into 1-inch cubes or $1/2$-inch-thick slabs and frozen in plastic zip-top bags
- Tempeh
- Minced garlic (mince several heads of garlic at once, spread it thinly in plastic zip-top bags, and freeze; snap off chunks when making sautés or soups)
- Fresh herbs (minced fresh and stored in a zip-top plastic baggie)

For a week's worth of ideas for how to use all this good stuff, see "Sample 7-Day Menu" on page 83.

Emphasizing Veggies

If you're not accustomed to buying and cooking vegetables, you might not know how to tell a fresh cabbage from one past its prime—or what to do with it once you've bought it. Here are a few common and tasty veggies to buy fresh at the grocery store and how to tell when they're good.

AVOCADOS
They're like butter, but they grow on a tree. An avocado is ripe when you squeeze it gently and feel a little bit of give, but no mushiness. Put slices on Mexican and Central American recipes, or spread it on toast with a sprinkle of salt and a squeeze of citrus juice.

BROCCOLI
Should be uniformly green with no yellow spots and no sliminess on the heads of the florets. Great raw, steamed, or in stir-fries.

CABBAGE
From Napa cabbage to Chinese cabbage, you're looking for firm, crisp, tight heads of leaves with

no wilting. Good in sautés and in some soups, but try to use it up the first time you cook it; it isn't as delicious in leftovers.

CARROTS
As long as they're not slimy, they're good! Munch on them raw dipped in peanut butter, hummus, or dressings as a snack, cook them with celery and onions in a soup base, or toss them with olive oil and salt and roast in the oven.

CELERY
Should be firm and crisp. It's a great dippable snack when raw, and good with carrots and onions as a soup base (aka *mirepoix* if you want to sound fancy).

KALE AND COLLARDS
These leafy vegetables should be crisp and green. If they are slimy or yellowed, they are past date. Remove the midrib before cooking. Steam the leaves until completely limp, then serve with a sauce. Or blanch for 60 seconds, drain, and sauté with garlic, olive oil, and a squirt of citrus juice.

MUSHROOMS

Should be moist but not soggy. Brown or crimini are more flavorful than button mushrooms and still affordable. Pricier varieties like portobello, maitake, chanterelle, and fresh shiitake are also tasty. Slice and sauté them over moderate heat with oil and a little bit of minced onion, garlic, or shallots.

PEAPODS

No matter the kind, they should have bright green, smooth, crisp pods. They may have some black "freckles"; these are normal. You can sauté them, steam them, or add them to noodle dishes.

POTATOES AND SWEET POTATOES

If they're firm and don't have sprouts or green spots, they're good. Roast them in the oven or cook them in the microwave.

TOMATOES

Fresh tomatoes are only really good in the summer. Eat as many as you can during peak season, and avoid their mealy out-of-season counterparts—with the notable exception of cherry and grape tomatoes, which grow well in greenhouses year-round. During the off-season, use canned tomatoes to make sauces and soups.

WINTER SQUASH (BUTTERNUT, ACORN)

Pick one that is heavy for its size, with smooth skin and no soft areas. Carefully cut it in half, remove the seeds, oil the interior, roast until tender, and scoop out the flesh to serve.

Where to Shop

Even if you live in a rural or suburban area, you can buy most of the food you need at a standard grocery store. Most grocery stores have a fresh produce area for fruits, veggies, and fresh herbs; dried and canned beans and big bags of rice in either an "ethnic foods" or "staples" aisle; spices in the baking aisle; a freezer section for frozen vegetables; and an eggs and dairy area, which may also offer plant milks and soy yogurt. Some stores will have a little health-foods section with mock meats and tofu . . . but you can usually get better prices and better products/flavors at specialty stores.

If you live in an urban area, you may have access to more options: health food stores or food co-ops, upscale "gourmet" stores, and more. If you're trying the foods of a specific ethnicity's cuisine, seek out shops catering to members of the community whose families have been cooking that food for centuries. Items will typically be cheaper and taste better. Pick up tahini and olive oil at a Middle Eastern market, tofu and stir-fry ingredients from an East Asian grocer, and Indian dals and spices from a South Asian shop.

Wherever you live, if you have access to farm stands or farmers markets, treat yourself to a few fresh, local veggies in-season when you can afford to. If brick-and-mortar stores in your area are lacking, shop online—from web-based spice stores to vegetarian specialty shops that will overnight you mock meats.

Secrets of the Bulk Bin

Bulk bins are the best way to buy dried goods because you can purchase as little or as much as you need. Sometimes packaged foods are available at one-third the price from bulk bins—you can get a better deal right in the same store! You pour from a dispenser or scoop from a bin, label the contents of your bag, and pay by weight at checkout. They're ubiquitous at Whole Foods and most food co-ops, but an ever-expanding list of mainstream grocery stores (Wegmans, WinCo, Kroger, etc.) offer them, too.

Common items in bulk bins:

- Whole grains
- Beans
- Lentils
- Flours
- Sweeteners
- Salt
- Dried fruits
- Nuts
- Snacks
- Coffee

Ways to store your bulk stuff at home:

- Show it off in wide-mouth screw-top glass jars on your shelves or in your pantry. What's prettier than a shelf full of dry beans?
- Stack it in plasticware.
- Pick up bigger bins at the dollar store.

No matter what container you choose, it should have a lid that you can close tightly (to prevent moths) and the material should be gnaw-proof (to deter mice). See pages 56–65 for how to cook some of your bulk-bin finds.

How to Cook Dried Beans

So you've saved a ton of money buying stuff from the bulk bins . . . but now how do you cook it? Don't worry—you'll be a pro in no time, whipping up delicious and nutritious meals with ease.

When cooking dried beans, you'll need to plan ahead. Dried beans must be soaked before cooking, so it's smart to prep a big batch once and plan for leftovers.

Step 1: Soaking

Some folks swear by an overnight soak, and others find a quick soak more convenient and equally tasty.

Overnight soak: Measure beans, put them in a bowl with enough cold, clean water to cover them by 2 inches, and soak them overnight (or for at least 8 hours). Larger beans need to soak longer than smaller ones.

Quick hot soak: Measure beans, put them in a pot with three times more water than beans, and bring to a boil. Then turn off the heat, cover, and let soak for 1 to 2 hours.

Step 2: Cooking

Rinse the beans, discarding the soaking liquid, and put them in a pot with at least three times more water than beans. Do not add salt or anything acidic at this point (it will toughen the beans' skin) but you can add spices, herbs, onion, garlic, ginger, and/or a strip of kombu seaweed (look for this online or in health-food stores) to make the beans more tender and flavorful.

Bring to a boil, then reduce heat and partially cover. Simmer until the beans are tender. The cook times on page 58 are typical, but start checking 15 minutes before the stated time. And know that older beans that have been sitting in your pantry for a year or two will take longer to cook.

TYPICAL COOKING TIMES AFTER SOAKING

Adzuki beans	1 hour
Black-eyed peas	1 hour
Cannellini beans	$1^1/_2$ hours
Cranberry beans	$1^1/_2$–2 hours
Chickpeas	2–3 hours
Great northern beans	$1^1/_2$–2 hours
Kidney beans	$1^1/_2$ hours
Lentils	20–30 minutes
Lima beans	$1^1/_2$ hours
Mung beans	45–60 minutes
Navy beans	$1^1/_2$ hours
Pinto beans	$1^1/_2$ hours
Split peas	1 hour

How to
Cook Grains

Here's a method that works for most whole grains (for how to cook bulgur and couscous, see page 62): Measure grains and clean cold water according to page 60, place both in a heavy-bottomed pot with a pinch of salt, and bring to a boil. Then reduce the heat to barely simmering and give the grains a stir. Start a timer and cover the pot tightly. Don't remove the lid until the cooking time is up! The steam generated by the simmer helps cook the grains.

For a tasty variation, try cooking grains in vegetable broth or carrot juice instead of water. Or add dried herbs and spices to the pot.

Grain Cooking Times

GRAIN
Amaranth
Pearled barley
Buckwheat
Millet
Quinoa
Red/Bhutanese rice
Brown rice
Black "forbidden" rice
White sushi rice
White regular rice
Wild rice
Wheat berries

RATIO OF GRAIN TO WATER	COOKING TIME
1 part grain to 3 parts water	25–30 minutes
1 part grain to 2.5 parts water	45–60 minutes
1 part grain to 2 parts water	15–20 minutes
1 part grain to 2.5 cups water	30 minutes
1 part grain to 1.75 parts water	12–15 minutes
1 part rice to 1.5 parts water	20 minutes
1 part rice to 2 parts water	45–50 minutes
1 part rice to 1.75 parts water	30 minutes
1 part rice to 1.75 parts water	15 minutes
1 part rice to 1.5 parts water	15–20 minutes
1 part rice to 3 parts water	40–45 minutes
1 part grain to 2 parts water	60–90 minutes

A Note on Cooking Bulgur and Couscous

Unlike other grains, bulgur (used in tabbouleh and other salads) and couscous (often served as a starchy complement to North African foods) have already undergone processing. Bulgur has been parboiled, dried, and cracked, and couscous is basically a tiny pasta. Both cook up quickly, so they're a great base for quick weeknight meals.

Bulgur: Use 2 parts water to 1 part grain. Place water in a small saucepan, bring to a boil, and then remove from heat. Add the bulgur and a pinch of salt, stir, and cover immediately. Let stand for 20 minutes, and then remove the lid. Ta-da! The bulgur will have absorbed all the hot water. Fluff with a fork and serve.

Couscous: Couscous is totally idiot-proof, so it's a great place to start if you're nervous in the kitchen. Use 1 part water to 1 part grain (keeping in mind that 1 cup dry couscous yields 4 cups cooked). Measure the dry stuff before the wet stuff so the couscous doesn't stick to your measuring cup. Place the water in a small saucepan, bring to a boil, and then remove from heat. Add the couscous and a pinch of salt, stir, and cover immediately. Let stand for 10 minutes, then remove the lid and fluff with a fork before serving.

A Trick for Cooking White Rice

Can't get the proportions right with white rice? If yours always ends up watery, or it dries out and burns, sticking to the bottom of the pot, you'll love this method. Trust me: you can make white rice the same way you cook pasta.

When you want to get fancy, try fussing with whether the rice is starchy or washed out. But for good general-purpose rice, this is a nice starting point:

1. Bring a 4-quart pot of water to a boil. Set a colander in your sink while you're waiting.

2. Add 1 cup of white rice, stir so that it doesn't stick to the bottom of the pot, and bring back to a lively boil. When the water starts boiling again, set a timer for 11 minutes.

3. When the timer sounds, drain the rice into the colander. Give the colander a good shake to get rid of excess water.

4. Empty the drained rice back into the pot, cover, and let stand for 5 minutes. The rice will finish cooking in its own steam.

Where to Save and Where to Splurge

Being vegetarian doesn't have to be pricey. The key is knowing when to keep the coins in your wallet and when shelling out a little more can make mealtimes extra delicious.

Always save on:

- Grains
- Beans
- Bulk foods
- Tofu
- Hard vegetables like carrots, potatoes, and butternut squash
- Apples and pears (in season)
- Peanut butter: Skip the jarred stuff and make your own! Buy roasted unsalted peanuts from the bulk bins and blend in a food processor for 5 to 10 minutes, until smooth.

With the money you save, I recommend always splurging on:

- Fresh fruits and vegetables. Learn how to pick them out (see page 48) and your favorite ways to cook and serve them. If you have a community-supported agriculture (CSA) share or farmers market in your area, take advantage of it.

- Good-quality soy sauce and your preferred condiments. A little goes a long way!

- Miso

- Good drizzling oils, like olive oil and toasted sesame oil

For special occasions, sometimes it makes sense to splurge on:

- Fresh herbs. A few leaves of fresh basil can transform a dish in a way that dried never will.

- Spices that you use in small quantities. You can get these for cheap at a natural foods store in bulk, at a south Asian grocer, or online from Penzeys. Find a few spices that you really love, and invest in the best quality you can afford.

COOKING

How to Read Recipes

You've nailed your grocery store trip. You've assembled your meat-free ingredients. But how do you cook the dang things? An online search will turn up lots of recipes for the same thing, and your local bookstore is likely full of cookbooks, so here's how to tell which ones to trust.

Online Recipes

- If you already have a few favorite cookbook authors, see where they're featured online.

- Websites associated with culinary magazines, or websites with a list of editorial staff, will have better quality control than personal blogs or general recipe-compendium-style sites.

- Look for a recipe's precision. Does it specify the size of the cuts, the level of heat to use, what the dish should smell and look like when it's done? Does the recipe say when to add salt? These details, plus positive reviews, are often indicators of a recipe that is worth a try.

- If you're perusing a food blog, check the comments on each post. This is the rare occasion when reading the comments *is* worth your time.

Cookbooks

- Check online reviews. Even if you prefer to buy in your local bookshop, seeing if something has (a) a lot of reviews, meaning it is heavily used, and (b) a lot of positive reviews will separate the good from the mediocre.

- Check reputable awards lists. The James Beard Awards have given the nod, or at least the nomination, to quite a few veg-friendly cookbooks over the years!

- As with online searches, check for precisely written recipes with specific, detailed instructions.

- Shop for cookbooks in bookstores where you trust the bookseller to know about food, or in trustworthy cookware stores that also stock cookbooks, such as Williams-Sonoma. Avoid the bargain bins. These are books you'll use every week, if not every day. Invest in something decent.

- Mainstream cookbook reviewing sites like the *New York Times* cookbook review column or the cookbook reviews on the *Kitchn* now regularly feature books with veg options.

- Know someone who's a good cook? Ask what cookbooks and authors they swear by.

How to Make Recipes Vegetarian

Eating vegetarian doesn't have to mean throwing away all your omnivorous cookbooks. To this day, some of my favorite cookbook authors—from Fuchsia Dunlop to Irma Rombauer Becker to Marcella Hazan—have never written a veg cookbook. Fortunately, it's easy to substitute for nonvegetarian ingredients. Of course, you can always use some of the cookbooks recommended at the end of this book to find a delicious vegetarian recipe (see Resources, page 137). But if you like a particular nonvegetarian recipe, don't be afraid to try it using meat substitutions (see page 76).

- **Is the meat blended in or used as a topping?** Substitute seasoned TVP (textured vegetable protein), store-bought faux beef crumbles, or even lentils seasoned with savory herbs and a dash of tamari to mimic the texture of ground beef.

- **Is the meat marinated or in a casserole?** The flavor interest is in the marinade or the casserole ingredients. Swap in frozen and thawed tofu (this is great for "chicken" cacciatore), simmer tempeh in the marinade, or soak seitan in it overnight. You're good to go.

- **Is it a sandwich filling?** You've got a fighting chance. Half the fun of a sandwich is in the condiments, anyway. Replace cold cuts and bacon with store-bought mock meat deli slices and veggie bacon. Instead of chicken salad, try fork-mashed chickpeas or tempeh that's been steamed for 10 minutes and then crumbled into chunks.

- **Is the meat in a broth?** Substitute veggie broth for beef, chicken, or pork broth in most instances, or buy vegetarian "chicken" and "beef" bouillon granules at health food stores. Or make your own chicken broth seasoning using equal amounts of dried onions, celery salt, white pepper, garlic powder, and mixed herbs like rosemary, parsley, or thyme. For a quick "beef" broth, boil 1 teaspoon of Chinese dried fermented black beans (not dried bulk-bin beans) in 2 quarts of water for 10 minutes, then strain out the solids before using.

- **If it's meat and almost nothing but,** like rump roast or steak, you might have to pass this one by, especially if the texture is essential to the dish. But if the meat serves more as a vehicle for the seasoning, you have a chance. Meat seasoned with a glaze, like beef bulgogi or teri-yaki chicken breast, can be replaced with large chunks of seitan (for beef) or chewy frozen and thawed tofu (for chicken).

- **If it's a fish dish,** that's a bit harder. In larger cities, grocers that cater to an Asian Buddhist community often sell frozen vegetarian mock fish. Does the recipe call for fish broth? Adding a sea vegetable like wakame or kelp could help. But like meat-centric dishes, if the fish is largely unadorned, look for another recipe.

- **Is it a turducken?** Yeah, you can even work with that. Stuff tempeh in tofu and wrap it in seitan slices. Never give up! Happy Thanks-Living, and cheers to your veg ingenuity.

How to Substitute Ingredients

To start, think about the function of an animal ingredient in a recipe. Is it adding flavor, texture, nutritional content, or even visual impact? For example, the beef in *boeuf bourguignon* provides a meaty texture, as well as a heavy dose of protein and plenty of fat to keep you full. In a burger, beef is a crumbly, high-protein, slightly smoky blank canvas for toppings. In a pho broth, it adds richness. Same ingredient, three different functions. That means you'll replace beef differently in a burger than in a pho broth.

Here's a practical example: a low-protein, low-fat grilled mushroom "burger" is going to leave you hungry 20 minutes after eating it, but simmering the same mushrooms with star anise and fermented dried black beans might be just the thing to flavor your pho broth. Conversely, simmering a lentil croquette in water and straining it out will give you total garbage for pho broth, but a lentil patty done just right makes a tasty and filling burger. You may need to substitute multiple things for a single nonvegetarian ingredient in order to land on a variation that really delivers the satisfaction you deserve.

With that in mind, shop for premade mock chik'n strips, fake bacon, beefless crumbles, premade veggie burgers, coconut coffee creamer, powdered egg substitute, etc., but don't be afraid to make your own. Homemade swaps cost less, aren't made in a factory, and sometimes don't even require extra time.

These "magic ingredients" will help you create flavorful meatless meals. Improvise away, or turn to page 83 for inspiration.

- **Ackee:** Eggy texture.
- **Avocados:** Creaminess. Great in smoothies, tacos, pan-seared as a foie gras stand-in, and—believe it or not—as an ingredient in chocolate mousse.
- **Banana puree:** Offers a little bit of moisture and binding in baked goods.
- **Beans and bean purees:** High in protein. Blending beans gives a starchy/creamy feel that can thicken dishes; lightly mashing them with a fork gives a texture similar to that of ground meat.

- **Chickpea flour:** Custardy texture, self-binding like eggs, high in protein. Just be sure to cook it enough to rid it of the raw flavor.
- **Chickpea water:** Also called aquafaba, this is the liquid that chickpeas are cooked or canned in. Whip with an electric whisk; it foams like egg whites. It can take only very gentle heat. Look online for tips on making vegan meringues, cheeses, or mayo with it.
- **Chinese fermented tofu:** Give dishes some of the tang and funk associated with gorgonzola or blue cheese. Find it in Asian grocery shops.
- **Cocoa powder:** Slight bitterness, charred edge, and deep, rich, earthy flavor. Try a pinch in a chili or hearty bean stew.
- **Coconut oil:** Offers satiety, creamy/fatty mouthfeel. The unrefined kind tastes like coconut; refined has a neutral flavor.
- **Dried mushrooms:** Meaty flavor, umami, depth and complexity of aroma, earthiness; great in a broth. If reconstituted and chopped, very assertive texture.
- **Earth Balance:** A common brand of butter substitute with a high fat content (think satiety!).

- **Fresh mushrooms:** Melting tenderness, depth and complexity of aroma. This is a low-protein and low-fat ingredient, meaning you'll need something else to provide long-burning fuel for your body.

- **Frozen and thawed firm tofu:** A knockout chicken substitute in stir-fries, soups, and casseroles. Freezing tofu makes it both firmer and more porous. It absorbs flavor beautifully and has an assertive texture. See page 107 for more on this technique.

- **Jackfruit:** Meaty texture.

- **Lentils:** Crumbly texture that still holds together; high in protein.

- **Liquid smoke:** This is literally liquefied hickory smoke. It's great for adding smoky and savory qualities.

- **Miso paste:** Imparts saltiness (like cured meats), umami savoriness, and richness of flavor.

- **Seaweed/nori/wakame:** Gives flavors of the sea. Wrap frozen and thawed tofu in it to make a "skin" around a mock fish dish, or grind some and add it to a mixture of rice vinegar, Chinese fermented tofu, and soy sauce to make a complex condiment that will stand in for Southeast Asian fish sauces.

- **Seitan:** High protein, toothsome meaty texture, absorbs flavorful broths well.
- **Smoked paprika:** Sweeter than liquid smoke and gently spicy. Stands in for the savoriness of cured meats.
- **Soft tofu:** High protein, binds baked goods, can be scrambled like eggs.
- **Soy sauce:** Umami, saltiness.
- **Sun-dried tomatoes:** Umami, brightness, acidity.
- **Walnuts:** Fatty, high in protein. When toasted, slightly smoky.

7 Basic Flavor Combos

It's helpful to have a few go-to flavor combinations inspired by your favorite cuisines that you can use as starting points for improvisations. Add the following spices to marinades, sprinkle them on top of grain, bean, or tofu dishes, or play with them while brainstorming menus.

1. **Mexican:** chilis, cilantro, coriander, cumin, oregano, onion, chili powder, garlic

2. **Middle Eastern:** lemon, coriander, sesame, thyme, sumac, parsley, garlic, mint

3. **North African:** paprika, cayenne, cumin, ginger, coriander, turmeric, white pepper

4. **Chinese:** garlic, ginger, soy sauce, chilis, black vinegar, scallions

5. **Greek:** oregano, rosemary, sage, thyme, mint, dill, parsley, cumin, black pepper

6. **Italian:** basil, oregano, sage, parsley, garlic, rosemary

7. **Thai:** shallots, garlic, fresh chilis, coriander, lemongrass, turmeric, galangal or ginger, Thai basil, lime

You don't have to stop here—develop your own favorite flavor combos. Cook intuitively by holding a few spices to your nose to see if they smell good together. If they taste good too, write down the combination so you can repeat it in the future. As beloved chef Julia Child once said, "Learn from your mistakes, be fearless, and above all have fun!"

Sample 7-Day Menu

At this point in the book, you know a bit about eating for health and making your way around the kitchen. Whether you're a culinary pro but new to meatless meals, or you're trying out cooking and vegetarianism at the same time, the week's worth of food suggestions that follow should give you starting points to develop your own menus of foods you love.

Cooking every day of the week might be practical if you feed a whole family or have people in the household who like to cook or help out. If it's too much for you, or if you're unaccustomed to cooking so much from scratch, start small. Pick one or two dishes from pages 84 through 90—say, those whose ingredients or flavors you know already—and give them a try. Cook in big batches and eat leftovers throughout the week. As your kitchen confidence grows, try cooking more from-scratch meals each week.

For online recipe sources and trusted cookbooks to help make dishes like these, see Resources on page 137.

Monday: Traditional American Fare

☞ **BREAKFAST** ☜
Orange juice or orange sections
Low-sugar, high-protein cereal with soy milk

☞ **LUNCH** ☜
Peanut butter and jelly sandwich
Carrot and celery sticks
Handful of potato chips

☞ **SNACK** ☜
Apple slices with peanut butter
GORP (trail mix) with chocolate, peanuts, and raisins

☞ **DINNER** ☜
Marinated roast seitan, baked tofu, or mock chicken
Spinach salad with walnuts, dried cranberries,
and mustard vinaigrette
Rice pilaf
Baked butternut squash

☞ **DESSERT** ☜
Chocolate cake

Tuesday: Hearty Health Food

→ **BREAKFAST** ←

Overnight oats with walnuts,
dried fruits, and chia seeds

Green smoothie with banana, soy milk, and a handful
of dark leafy greens (kale, collards, or chard)

Tea/coffee

→ **LUNCH** ←

Microwaved sweet potato with black beans and salsa

Baked tortilla chips

→ **SNACK** ←

Date and cashew bars

→ **DINNER** ←

Brown rice bowl with teriyaki-baked tofu
and crispy shiitake mushrooms

Mesclun salad with sunflower seeds, chickpeas, tomatoes, shredded purple cabbage, and tahini dressing

→ **DESSERT** ←

Apple brown Betty

Wednesday: Middle Eastern Menu

→ BREAKFAST ←
Ful medames (fava beans)
garnished with plain yogurt
Pita bread

→ LUNCH ←
Lentil soup
Steamed spinach with a squeeze of lemon juice
Pita chips and hummus

→ SNACK ←
Handful of pistachios
Sweet mint tea

→ DINNER ←
Tomato, red onion, and cucumber salad with
feta or lemon-oregano marinated tofu
Rice or bulgur wheat and lentils with caramelized
onion (top with yogurt if desired)

→ DESSERT ←
Halvah sesame candy

Thursday: Taste of East Asia

❧ BREAKFAST ❧

Rice and mung bean congee (rice porridge) with toasted sesame oil, soy sauce, and chopped scallions

❧ LUNCH ❧

Tofu pad thai

❧ SNACK ❧

Fried broad beans

Orange sections

Green tea

❧ DINNER ❧

Panfried tempeh strips

White rice with *gado-gado* peanut sauce

Collard greens stewed in coconut milk with turmeric, shallots, chili paste, and lemongrass

❧ DESSERT ❧

Fresh coconut

Friday: Tour of Central America

✣ BREAKFAST ✣

Huevos (or tofu) *a la Mexicana* (scrambled
with sautéed onions, tomatoes, oregano, and
chili peppers) with warm tortillas

✣ LUNCH ✣

Crispy corn tortillas or hard taco shells split in half
(pack separately so they don't get mushy)

Vegetarian refried beans

Shredded crisp lettuce

Chunky tomato salsa or pico de gallo

✣ SNACK ✣

Tortilla chips with *sikil pak* (traditional Mayan dip
made with roasted vegetables and pumpkin seeds)

✣ DINNER ✣

Black bean soup topped with avocado slices

Corn bread

Sautéed spinach with lemon, cumin, and oregano

✣ DESSERT ✣

Mango con chile y limón (sliced mango with a squeeze
of lime, a pinch of salt, and a dash of chili powder)

Saturday: Soul Food Inspired

✦ BREAKFAST ✦
Cheesy grits with sautéed Swiss chard and
roasted cherry tomatoes
Fried veggie sausage
Biscuits with mushroom gravy
Sliced fresh fruit
Strawberry banana smoothie

✦ LUNCH ✦
Mac and cheese or nutritional yeast "cheeze" sauce
Sweet potato oven fries
Fresh okra sautéed with garlic

✦ SNACK ✦
Spiced boiled peanuts

✦ DINNER ✦
Breaded and fried seitan
Citrus collard greens
Skillet corn bread

✦ DESSERT ✦
Red velvet cake

Sunday: Deluxe Weekend Comfort Food

⟶ **FANCY BRUNCH** ⟵

Hash browns

Tofu scramble/scrambled eggs with onions,
red peppers, and basil

⟶ **LUNCH** ⟵

Grilled cheese or "cheeze" with tomato slices, onion,
pickles, sauerkraut, and/or veggie bacon

Tomato soup

Side salad

Chocolate chip cookies

⟶ **SNACK** ⟵

Wheat crackers with almond butter and banana slices

⟶ **DINNER** ⟵

Minestrone soup

Orecchiette pasta with walnuts, chickpeas,
and escarole or broccoli rabe

Sautéed mushrooms with garlic, parsley, and lemon zest

Simple green salad with olive oil and red wine vinegar

⟶ **DESSERT** ⟵

Almond cookies and decaf coffee

Hearty Breakfasts and Brunches

You're going to need options whether you're powering up for busy mornings or slowing down on lazy weekends. You already know about toast and peanut butter, granola and yogurt, and buying veggie bacon to go with your pancakes, but have you considered these?

- **Protein bites:** In a food processor, blend pitted dates, coconut, raw cashews, and chocolate-flavored protein powder. Keep adding dates until the mixture binds together. Roll the mixture into 1-inch balls and then toss in more protein powder or coconut flakes to keep them from sticking together.

- **Oatmeal** won't stick to your ribs too long on its own, so stir in some peanut butter, slivered almonds, pecans, walnuts, or toasted hazelnuts for staying power. Allergic to nuts? Try adding soy milk or tahini.

- **Savory breakfast porridges** made of rice or millet, sometimes cooked with beans to make a complete protein, are popular in some parts of the world.

- **Chickpea omelets:** Whisk chickpea flour with water and a pinch of salt and cook in a hot pan until the batter is set, the glossiness has just disappeared from the top, and the bottom is crisp but not burnt—just like cooking pancakes. The result is custardy, like eggs, and can be stuffed with your favorite omelet fillings. Gluten-free, soy-free, and vegan, chickpea omelets are great for a crowd. Look for recipes online.

- **Scramble tofu** with nutritional yeast, pink salt, miso paste, turmeric, and your favorite veggies. Serve with toast.

Inspired Sandwich Lunches

Nothing makes a quick and tasty lunch like a hearty sandwich. Get inspired by this list and then search for recipes or improvise your own tasty fillings.

- Bean spreads, like hummus, white bean and rosemary spread, and walnut-lentil-miso pâté
- Chickpea salad (great in a pita)
- Tempeh salad with mayo or veggie mayo (chicken salad style)
- Mock meat slices
- Marinated and baked tempeh
- Sliced cheese, sandwich veggies, and pickles
- Classic PB&J with peanut butter and strawberry jam
- Fancy nut butter and jam: Mix it up with fancy bread, cashew or almond butter, and gourmet fruit spreads
- Classic hot eggplant parmigiana sandwich with tomato sauce and mozzarella

- Vietnamese-style tofu banh mi: Simmer tofu in soy sauce, grated fresh ginger, rice vinegar, and sugar. Fill a baguette with the cooked and seasoned tofu, along with sliced cucumbers, julienned carrots, cilantro sprigs, and sriracha.

- Veggie muffaletta: Use mock meat slices and a spread of olives chopped with giardiniera-pickled celery, cauliflower, and carrot.

- Niçoise-inspired baguette with white bean puree, roasted red peppers, kalamata olives, parsley, mustard, red onions, and lettuce.

Bag Snacks

Lots of folks report that the most challenging time to stay vegetarian is when they're out and about with their tummy rumbling and nothing veg-friendly to eat. If you make a habit of packing a portable snack, potentially difficult situations like a car trip to an unfamiliar town or a longer-than-usual night at the office won't be a problem.

The best snacks are nonperishable, lightweight, high-satiety (meaning they'll keep you full for a while), and mostly crush-proof, so you can keep them on hand (or at the bottom of a bag) for months, until a craving strikes. A little container of the following snacks in your purse, backpack, desk, or car will keep you feeling full until your next meal.

Simple snacks you can find at any grocer:

- Trail mix
- Sunflower seeds
- Peanuts, cashews, almonds, pistachios, or your favorite nut mix
- Peanut-butter-filled pretzels

- Cereal (look for varieties with a higher protein-to-carbs ratio)

Homemade bites (search for recipes online):

- Tamari almonds
- Oven-roasted chickpeas
- Coconut peanut butter balls
- Date and cashew bars
- Almond-fig balls

Any of the above are tasty, satisfying options. But if you have access to a health food store, specialty market, or Asian grocer, seek out these extra-special snacks:

- Savory "jerky" snacks, like Primal Strips and Stonewall's Jerquee
- Toasted coconut chips
- Protein and granola bars
- Flavored roasted chickpeas
- Chia seeds (dissolve a couple tablespoons in fruit juice for a filling snack high in omega-3s)
- Spiced nuts
- Sesame sticks

- "Chunks of Energy" snack bites
- Roasted broad beans
- Spiced tofu and tempeh snacks
- Dried tofu
- Wasabi peas

Flavor Bases

Creating full-flavored dishes will make committing to a vegetarian diet even easier—not to mention more delicious. Both of the following techniques involve cooking a flavorful ingredient in fat at the start of a dish, building the core flavor. (See pages 100–105 for how to use them in recipes.)

Sautéing Aromatics

Sautéing vegetables, spices, and herbs—known as *aromatics*—in oil infuses the oil with rich aromas that will carry through to the final dish. Aromatics vary worldwide; here are a few to get you started:

- Thai cooking uses shallots, garlic, and chilis
- Middle Eastern cooking uses garlic, onions, tomatoes, and scallions
- Latin cooking uses garlic, onions, bell peppers, and tomatoes
- French cooking uses onions, carrots, and celery
- Indian cooking uses onions, garlic, chilis, and ginger

Blooming Spices

Some of the flavor compounds in dried spices dissolve in water, but others come out only when they're dissolved in oil. Most beans, grains, fruits, and veggies are low in fat, so they won't ooze grease in the pan the way meat does. Sizzling spices in oil at the start of a recipe—aka *blooming* the spices—before you throw in other ingredients will give the dish the same flavor-infused quality of a meat-based dish. (Frying in oil before adding water allows both the water-soluble and the fat-soluble flavors to come out.)

Try blooming any of the following:

- cumin
- mustard seeds
- red pepper flakes
- thyme
- rosemary
- powdered garlic
- ginger
- curry powders

How to Make an Awesome Bean Soup

Making a great bean soup is simple! Most soups start with a flavor base, then call for beans and veggies cooked until tender. This general method starts with sautéing aromatics and allows for plenty of improvisation. Add a grain if you want a complete protein in a bowl, or serve the soup with bread, rice, quinoa, or millet pilaf on the side.

1. Get a big pot. Add some oil, such as olive, canola, or vegetable oil. Place over medium heat.

2. Add chopped alliums—any combination of garlic, onion, leeks, shallots, etc.—and cook, stirring, until they are soft, pale yellow, and fragrant, about 3 to 5 minutes.

3. Add spices and dried (not fresh) herbs. Try a pinch of black pepper, red pepper flakes, cumin seeds, dried parsley, or your favorite packaged spice blend (or use any of the 7

Basic Flavor Combos, page 81). Cook spices in the oil for 60 to 90 seconds.

4. Add chopped veggies and grains, according to their cooking times, along with a pinch of salt.

   * **Hard, long-cooking veggies** like carrots, yams, celery, potatoes, turnips, and parsnips: 12–15 minutes

   * **Medium-cooking veggies** like canned tomatoes, cabbage, escarole, kale, and collards: 8–10 minutes

   * **Grains:** 10–45 minutes depending on type (see pages 60–61)

   * **Quick-cooking veggies** like delicate leafy greens, sprouts, and tender young mushrooms: 2 minutes or less

5. Add water or stock with hard veggies, turn up the heat, bring to a boil, and then lower to a simmer. Add canned or cooked beans when you add medium-cooking veggies.

6. When all the vegetables and grains are tender, take the pot off the heat. Add fresh herbs, additional salt, and even a dash of tamari to round out the flavor. Eat and enjoy!

How to Make Amazing Stir-Fry

Like bean soup, stir-fry is nutritious, easy to make, quick, and endlessly customizable. Always prepare your ingredients ahead of time—stir-fries come together fast! Chop the veggies (small, so they cook quickly), mince the garlic, and measure the liquid ingredients. If using hard vegetables that need to cook for a long time, like winter squash or tough greens, cook them briefly in simmering water before starting the stir-fry (this is known as blanching); otherwise, they won't be tender in the final dish.

1. Start with a large wok. A crowded wok means a badly cooked stir-fry. Place over high heat and warm for about 30 seconds.

2. Add a tablespoon or two of neutral-tasting oil that can handle high heat, such as peanut oil, coconut oil, canola oil, or mixed vegetable oil.

3. Add aromatics, such as minced garlic, ginger, and maybe some minced shallots. Sauté these until they make the room smell great. This will probably take less than a minute—don't burn them! If you want to add dried chilis or a flavor paste, such as *sambal oelek* or chili bean paste, do so now and fry for another 15 to 30 seconds.

4. Add tofu (firm-pressed, frozen and thawed, or fried puffs), seitan bits, or mock meats.

5. Start adding vegetables: shredded carrots, mushrooms, slivered onions, and tough greens go in first. Keep tossing them with a wooden spoon so they don't stick to the wok. You might even add a little vegetable stock or soy sauce diluted 50/50 with water, which will braise, soften, and flavor the veggies.

6. Once the firmer ingredients have softened, add tender ingredients like peppers or spinach. Cook while stirring.

7. Finally, kill the heat, add a little stir-fry sauce if you like, and top with any or all of the following:

   • minced scallions
   • a little toasted sesame oil
   • crispy fried onions
   • fresh herbs like Thai basil or cilantro

8. Serve over rice or Asian noodles for a quick, healthy, and filling meal!

How to Make Tofu Delicious

Let's have a word about tofu, shall we?

People in the U.S. have been hating on tofu for decades now, calling it bland, gross, or a poor substitute for meat. As if that's not enough, plenty of "health food" cookbooks will steer you in the wrong direction when it comes to tofu prep. But tofu's got a distinguished culinary history in Asia, where people have been making delicious bean curd dishes for centuries—dishes that even omnivores eat with relish!

Tofu comes in several varieties, which are suitable for different purposes. Standard grocery stores typically sell two types:

Firm: good for freezing and thawing to use in marinades or in stir-fries; deep-frying in cubes; and slicing thin and baking.

Silken: good in miso soup and, to some extent, creamy dressings.

At an Asian market, you'll likely find a wider range, with more variations in texture and flavor. The following are great in stir-fries:

- Shreds
- Pressed and flavored
- Pressed and fried
  (sometimes called "tofu steak")
- Puffs
- Fresh
- Water-packed

Beyond stir-fries, seek out tofu recipes by writers who are trained in fine East Asian cooking, such as Fuchsia Dunlop, or try these techniques, which are good with the firm and water-packed variety.

Frozen and Thawed Tofu

A lot of cookbooks tell you to press tofu before adding to a recipe. Substitute this stuff, and you may just make the first tofu you've ever truly loved. You'll almost never go wrong by having a freezer full of it. Drain the tofu (no need to blot it dry), slice it into 1-inch cubes or $1/2$-inch slabs, and then freeze it in plastic bags. It develops a meaty, chewy texture, soaks up marinades like a fiend, and is spectacular in casseroles, stir-fries, and bakes. Pull it out on busy weeknights and thaw it in the same amount of time it takes to press tofu in a colander.

Baked Tofu

Baked tofu is one of the two great temporal lies of cookbooks. (What's the other? "Cook the onions for 10 minutes." Cooking them for 30 minutes will invariably result in a better recipe.) Tofu starts to look good after 20 minutes, but baking it for 40 to 60 minutes will result in a pleasantly chewy texture. Baked tofu is great for topping salads.

Preheat the oven to 375°F. Cut a standard block of tofu once lengthwise and then into 1-inch-thick slabs. Make a marinade of 2 parts soy sauce, 4 parts rice vinegar, 1 part sriracha, and a dash of sesame oil. Put the tofu in a tempered glass baking pan and pour in the marinade until it barely covers the tops of the slices. Bake for 40 to 60 minutes, turning every 10 minutes, until it looks delicious.

5 Great Bacon Substitutes

If you're missing bacon, chances are you're craving some combination of saltiness, smokiness, chewiness, fattiness, and savoriness—probably not the cruelty! In addition to mock bacon strips, try getting your fix from one of these:

1. **Commercial "bacon bits" sold as salad toppings.** Salty, crunchy, and with a meaty flavor, these are great as a garnish for green salads or sprinkled on pasta or potato salads. They're also good in recipes for sweet-and-savory cookies, scones, or shortbread. Many versions are just texturized soy protein, salt, and vegetarian flavor extracts. Check the printed ingredients list to ensure that they're veg-friendly . . . and don't confuse them for health food!

2. **Tempeh bacon.** This makes a juicy, chewy, smoky bacon substitute. Slice tempeh into strips, or crumble to make faux bacon bits,

and panfry with a mixture of soy sauce, smoked paprika, brown sugar, apple cider vinegar, and neutral-tasting oil until the liquid evaporates.

3. **Coconut bacon.** If you're missing the fat of bacon, coconut is your answer. Toss large-flake unsweetened coconut in a sauce that's equal parts neutral oil, soy sauce/tamari, maple syrup, apple cider vinegar, and liquid smoke (or a pinch of smoked paprika). Bake on a lined baking sheet at 350°F for 10 to 15 minutes, turning every couple of minutes and keeping a close watch—this recipe goes from golden to blackened very quickly!

4. **Smoked salt.** This stuff is a great swap for bacon that is used as an ingredient in a dish, like in collard greens, or a condiment (there's even a commercial version called Bacon Salt). Other swaps that add salty, smoky, rich flavors: ancho or chipotle chilis, beverages like lapsang souchong tea or rauschbier (great in stews or braises), or a dash of liquid smoke.

5. **Shiitake mushroom bacon.** If you like your bacon chewy instead of crispy, this one is for you. Clean and halve $1/2$ pound of shiitake mushrooms, and then toss them with 2 tablespoons of olive oil, 1 teaspoon of tamari, $1/4$ teaspoon of salt, 1 teaspoon of brown sugar, and $1/2$ teaspoon of smoked paprika. Marinate for 30 minutes, and then transfer to an ovenproof dish. Bake at 350°F for 40 to 60 minutes, turning every 10 minutes or so, until mushrooms are brown and chewy.

Umami Hacks

If you're like many vegetarians, you'll probably feel occasional pangs for foods you've given up. Missing meat may be a sign that you're low on protein, iron, or other essential nutrients, or that you're craving saltiness, fattiness, "meaty" mouthfeel, smokiness, or "savoriness," aka umami.

Umami, along with sweetness, sourness, bitterness, and saltiness, is one of the basic flavors. Often described as a savory, meaty taste, it is correlated with a general sense of deliciousness. It's a common flavor in meat as well as in meatless foods that contain glutamate, such as:

- Oil-cured black olives
- Miso
- Fermented tofu
- Sun-dried tomatoes or tomato paste
- Tangy cultured nut spreads
- Nutritional yeast
- Asafetida (a spice used in Indian cuisine)
- Chinese fermented black beans

- West African fermented beans such as *dawa dawa* and *gari*
- Soy sauce or tamari
- *Ume* plum vinegar
- Dried porcini or shiitake mushrooms
- Kombu and nori seaweed
- Cumin and smoked paprika

Feed your next craving with any of the above, or try one of these combinations:

- Seitan with capers
- Bread topped with smashed avocado and smoked paprika
- Miso soup with chewy tofu
- Smoked almonds
- VLT sandwich made with veggie bacon, good quality bread, and avocado

If you need to, reread "Reasons to Feel Awesome" (page 18) and remind yourself of your motivation. Are you making these choices for your health? For the health of the animals? For the health of the planet? You can do this. One meal at a time.

How Not to Be Hungry 24/7

When you decide to cut meat from your diet, it's an easy mistake to replace it strictly with starchy carbohydrates like bread and pasta. And although meat has a lot of things in (and associated with) it that you don't want, it is also rich in fat and protein, which your body digests more slowly than carbohydrates. As a result, new vegetarians often experience hunger more quickly and more often. Cravings can also be a sign that you're low on calcium and iron-rich plant foods. If you find your stomach grumbling seemingly all the time, ask yourself:

- **Are you eating enough fat and protein?** A moderate amount of fat is your friend, and you definitely want to make sure you're getting enough protein. Emphasize unprocessed, nutrient-dense sources like seeds, nuts, tempeh, beans, and moderate amounts of oils with monounsaturated fats.

- **Are you snacking?** It's a good idea to have a healthy snack between your main meals. Whole nuts and seeds or veggie sticks with bean dip are great choices. Don't let yourself go hungry.

- **Are you truly hungry?** Make sure you're not angry, lonely, tired, or just having a craving for a particular food—a lot of people mistake strong emotions for a need to eat. Or just plain thirsty. Take good care of yourself on every front!

- **Are you craving a specific flavor?** Check the nutrients in the thing you're missing—in addition to protein, it could be calcium or iron, and there are plant-derived sources for that. Leafy greens like kale and collards will often make your body feel great.

Living the

VEGETARIAN
LIFE

Handling Tough Situations with Grace

Okay, you've got your diet plan figured out . . . and then other people come into the picture. When your food choices clash with those of the people you work, live, and hang out with, navigating familiar situations gets a bit trickier, though hardly impossible.

Home Situations

- If you live with people who eat meat, try to find favorite dishes that are already vegetarian, such as pasta with marinara sauce, tomato soup and grilled cheese, or veggie stir-fry.

- Don't lose touch with your family recipes! Modifying and retaining treasured cooking traditions is a great way to show respect to older family members who might see your vegetarianism as a rejection. Definitely try to retain what you can of your history. (See the substitutions on page 76 for ways to make existing recipes vegetarian.)

- If you have a non-veg spouse or partner, work together to find (and cook!) meatless dishes you both enjoy. Consider setting some ground rules—for example, you won't keep meat in the house, but it's fine for your partner to eat meat at restaurants—and remember to be flexible.

Work Situations

- There's a time for veg evangelism and a time to let things be, especially when your paycheck is at stake. Off the job, be an advocate if you want, but when you're on the clock, don't be "that guy."

- If coworkers are going to sass you about being vegetarian, or just express some curiosity about your diet, there's no need to make a big deal out of it. Answer any questions you receive simply and politely. "It's a quinoa and chick-pea salad. Would you like to try a bite?" goes over a lot better than "It's my vegetarian lunch because I think meat is murder." (You may think that, but people will come around on their own terms!)

- Pack lunches that work with the kitchen tools and appliances available to you. Fresh salads and perishable leftovers are great if you can store them in a fridge, but if all you have is a microwave and a can opener, bring canned bean soups. Nut butter sandwiches will keep without refrigeration for a few hours.

Social Situations

- **At a dinner party:** When you're invited, tell the host that you're vegetarian and would love to bring a dish to share. That way, you'll have at least one thing to eat!

- **At a cookout:** If the grill is going to have meat on it and you don't want your food in contact with the same surface, wrap some veggies and tofu cubes with a marinade inside a foil packet, and then place the packet on the grill when it's cooking time.

- **Hosting a party:** If you're veg for ethical reasons, you're not obligated to serve foods that are contrary to your morals . . . but as a good host, you're obligated to serve foods your guests will enjoy! Lots of common party snacks are vegetarian: pretzels, popcorn, chocolate, mixed nuts, cheese and crackers, hummus and veggies, chips and dips, and more. And no doubt you have guests who love lasagnas, salads, pizza, and chili and corn bread. Find out what your guests' favorite foods and flavors are. Or consider hosting a themed potluck:

  + **Taco bar:** Set out a bunch of fillings for tacos, or assign a filling to each friend, and see who comes up with the best combo.

  + **Roll your own sushi:** Make a big batch of sushi rice and have everyone bring a veg maki filling. Have a few rolling mats and knives. Make a pot of miso soup to serve on the side while everyone rolls and slices.

  + **Pizza potluck:** You supply the crusts and sauce, guests bring different toppings, and everyone tops their own personal pie.

- **Cookbook party:** Got a few friends who all love the same cookbook, but it's too pricey (or complicated) for you to cook a whole meal out of alone? Have friends coordinate dishes from the cookbook to make and bring to build a fancy feast.

4 Little White Lies

Honesty, the saying goes, is the best policy. But we all inevitably find ourselves in situations when a quick excuse is the most effective form of communication. Maybe it's an overbearing relative, a colleague or professional contact, or someone you just don't know well. When you don't want to eat a non-veg food, try saying:

- "I'm allergic to that."
- "I'm recovering from food poisoning."
- "I'm stuffed."
- "I'm doing a diet challenge with friends, and I can't eat that."

Plus one dodge and one truth: If a fib doesn't sit right with you, simply say, "No, thank you." And of course, honesty is an option, and you might be surprised by how well your comment is received. With time, it gets easier to say: "Oh, thank you. It's so kind of you to offer, but I'll pass. I prefer to stick to vegetarian options—would you happen to have anything meatless?"

Dining Out as a Vegetarian

The next time your friends whine about having to go to some rabbit food hippie restaurant to make you happy, be brave, be bold, and eat well! The world of veggie options is bigger and richer than you're imagined. And who knows? Your tabbouleh and falafel platter might just look so good next to your friend's overcooked chicken breast that the next time you two go back, she'll decide to have what you're having.

Region-Specific Restaurants

- **Middle Eastern** or "Mediterranean" gets you tabbouleh, hummus, falafel, *fattoush* (a bread salad made with pita), and lentil soup.

- **North African** food (Moroccan, Tunisian) should have couscous, chickpea dishes, and, if you're lucky, veggie *harira*, a flavorful soup with legumes and spices.

- **Ethiopian** cuisine has you covered with all sorts of *wots*—bean and vegetable stews—that are rich in flavor and nutrition. And everything is served on top of protein-dense injera, a pleasantly tangy flatbread.

- **Indian** is another good option. North Indian cuisine should have a full vegetarian section on the menu, and South Indian food is almost unfailingly veg-friendly.

- **Caribbean Islands** cuisine should give you options, with plenty of flavor to boot. Jamaica even has its own vegan-friendly health food tradition known as Ital food, part of the Rastafarian philosophy. Look for options ranging from steamed pumpkin and curried greens to spicy seitan, tofu, and soy protein.

- **Central and South American** places can hook you up with delicious veg meals. The ancient Aztecs and Mayans had the smart idea to treat corn with lime (known as nixtamalization), which makes the protein more accessible to the body. The result? Combine corn tortillas or rice with refried beans or black beans, and you've got a complete protein. Note that some restaurants cook their beans with lard.

- **East Asian** restaurants generally have something to offer.

  - **Japanese:** Try avocado maki and edamame. Look out for fish—which may be labeled as bonito—in the soup broth.

  - **Korean:** Try the vegetable bibimbap, but check for anchovies in the kimchi or the *kochujang*/hot sauce—claiming a spurious seafood allergy can help if your server is in a rush, since even the busiest kitchen doesn't want to kill a customer!

  - **Chinese** cuisine can offer great tofu and vegetable dishes. Steer clear of meat-broth-based sauces and oyster sauce, both of which can show up in seemingly veg dishes. It doesn't hurt to ask if the food has "meat flavor" or is "suitable for a Buddhist diet." Due to cultural differences, some people will hear "meat" and think "visible chunks," not "any meat content in any form."

- **Vietnamese:** Look forward to fresh veggie and herb spring rolls, lemongrass tofu over rice noodles, a tofu banh mi sandwich, and more. Just ask for no fish sauce, and be aware that the same warnings about meat broths in Chinese restaurants apply here, especially in soups. Happily, due to Vietnam's large Buddhist population, most establishments are familiar with the requirements of a vegetarian diet, and if you hit a language barrier, the word *chay*, in a flat tone, means "vegetarian."

- **Thai** food works, too—just ask them to hold the fish sauce and shrimp paste. Red curry with vegetables and tofu in coconut milk is a reliable option.

- **European-style** restaurants provide more of a challenge, but from Polish potato pierogis to Russian kasha, from Greek spanakopita to German *käsespätzle* and *spinatknödel*, and from Italian *pasta al pomodoro* to side salads most anywhere, you should be able to find something that fits your needs.

Other Restaurants

Most restaurants, even steakhouses, are likely to offer at least salad and bread, and maybe bean soup. Don't be shy about asking for off-menu options; many restaurants have an unlisted vegetarian/vegan option. Likewise, you'd be surprised at how many breakfast buffets have soy milk if you ask for it.

At a diner, you've always got French fries, all-day oatmeal, or grilled cheese. Nearly every American-style restaurant, from local dives to upscale gastropubs, now offers a veggie burger.

If you're researching choices in advance, the "chain restaurant vegetarian options" Google search is your friend! Even McDonald's has yogurt parfaits and salads.

Note that some restaurants will use the same cooking equipment for meats and vegetarian dishes; ask your server about cross-contamination if you're concerned.

Traveling as a Vegetarian

Headed on an adventure? If you'll be taking a flight on which a meal is served, call the airline and ask for a special vegetarian option. You'll usually need to place your request at least 72 hours in advance. Here are some standard meal codes used by all airlines worldwide. Note that not all carriers offer every option, but VLML and VGML are almost universally available.

- **AVML: Asian vegetarian meal.** A lacto-vegetarian meal flavored with spices from the Indian subcontinent. Could be spicy.

- **FPML: fruit platter meal.** Contains only fresh fruit.

- **RVML: vegetarian raw meal.** A vegan meal that contains only raw vegetables and salads.

- **VGML: vegetarian vegan meal.** A meal with no animal-derived products.

- **VJML: vegetarian Jain meal.** An Indian-spiced vegan meal prepared according to Jain religious restrictions—contains only vegetables grown aboveground and fruit.

- **VLML: vegetarian lacto-ovo meal.** A meal with no fish or meat, with typical "middle American" flavors. May contain eggs and dairy.

- **VOML: vegetarian Oriental meal.** A vegan meal prepared in a Chinese style.

If you're traveling to a country where you don't speak the local language, these resources will help you explain your diet to other people:

- **The Vegan Passport** from the UK's Vegan Society features an explanation of what vegans do and don't eat in more than ninety languages.

- **Smartphone apps** like V Cards serve a similar function, showing translated "I am vegetarian" explanations. Just remember that the apps live on your smartphone and not in a paper book. Beware the "low battery" warning!

- **Google Translate** can help you draft a list of what you do and don't eat, including general categories as well as the regional foods of your destination. Print four copies to a sheet and stash them in pockets, baggies, and luggage. Include a big translated PLEASE at the top of the page and THANK YOU at the bottom, a translation of "I am vegetarian," and your food lists under "yes" and "no" headings.

- **HappyCow.net** lists veg-friendly restaurants worldwide, from Aarhus to Zlin. Yelp and TripAdvisor can also help in some locations.

- Several tour companies offer package tours worldwide for vegetarians, as well as a vegetarian cruise and many vegetarian spas, but none of these come cheap.

5 Stealthy Nonvegetarian Foods

At this point, you've hopefully found some new foods you love, whether you're cooking them yourself or scouring your surroundings for delicious vegetarian-friendly restaurants. You're feeling good about the choices you're making. Don't let these five sneaky items derail your efforts.

1. **Worcestershire sauce:** This condiment and seasoning contains anchovies. Avoid not only the sauce, but foods and drinks it often goes into, like Chex Mix and Bloody Marys.

2. **Gelatin:** Made from boiled skins and tendons, it shows up in commercial fruity gelatin desserts, marshmallows, many chewy fruit candies, pill capsule coatings, and some margarines.

3. **Broths and stocks:** If you're dining out, be aware that some restaurants cook vegetarian-looking foods in beef, pork, or chicken broth.

Ask if you're unsure. Even tofu dishes at Chinese restaurants are often braised in a meat stock, but many kitchens can substitute water or veggie broth upon request.

4. **"Natural flavorings":** This phrase found on many American food packages can refer to foods of either vegetable or animal origin. When in doubt, contact the manufacturer or search online to see if someone else has recently researched the product.

5. **Carmine/natural red #4/cochineal:** This ingredient, used as food coloring and in lipstick, is made from powdered insects.

Despite the best intentions, we all make mistakes from time to time. Try not to worry too much about this stuff; we're trying to make better choices in a sometimes-screwy world, not be so perfect that we burn all our energy keeping an immaculate vegetarian diet. If you accidentally eat one of these ingredients, don't stress out—just avoid it next time. This isn't a purity contest.

Acquired Tastes (and How to Acquire Them)

Two stumbling blocks that vegetarians face are disliking new foods and finding themselves in a rut. The solution? Put your mind to acquiring a taste! With a bit of effort and the following tips, you'll find yourself falling in love with unfamiliar foods and maybe even something you thought you hated, whether that's tofu or broccoli. A few things are key:

- **Preparation matters.** If you're tasting a dish for the first time, make sure it has been prepared well. Certain foods—like eggplant or tofu— can be delicious or repulsive depending on whether they're prepared properly. Try a new dish at a restaurant that is famous for making that food, or get a well-reviewed cookbook and follow the recipe precisely until you've mastered it.

- **Quality matters.** The first time you taste a food, try to get it from the best possible source so that it's top quality. Think about the difference between an in-season tomato fresh from the garden and a pale, mealy winter tomato trucked in from far away.

- **Cultivate open-mindedness.** Don't try to make the food something other than what it is. You wouldn't eat an apple slice, knowing that it's an apple, and criticize it for being a terrible orange, right? Similarly, don't try miso-tahini sauce and be disappointed that it's not beef gravy. Be in the present moment with the food that's in front of you, and try to directly experience the unique taste and texture. Keep an open mind, and think of yourself as a curious person on a tiny adventure outside your comfort zone.

- **Compare and contrast.** Once you've tasted the dish, you'll notice some similarities to and differences from other foods. Without labeling these qualities as good or bad, make a mental note of them, much like you would at a wine tasting.

- **Don't expect to like it.** In fact, expect to have a negative reaction the first time you taste something and be willing *not* to convince yourself you'll hate it forever. Most people dislike tea or coffee or olives or wine on first taste, but look at how many people develop an appreciation for them.

- **Go slow.** Research shows that familiarity is a key aspect of liking. Expect that you may need ten or fifteen exposures in order to develop a taste for something. Go gradually—sample a bit once a week for six months. If you still hate it, it might just not be for you. But . . .

- **Don't lose heart!** The more things you try and (eventually) enjoy, the more pleasure you'll get out of life!

RESOURCES

Health and Nutrition

Vegetarian Nutrition
Evidence-based information from the Vegetarian Nutrition Dietetic Practice Group.
vegetariannutrition.net

The Vegan RD
Approachable food and supplementation advice from registered dietitian and animal lover Ginny Kisch Messina.
theveganrd.com

No Meat Athlete
Recipes, workout plans, and book recommendations from a plant-powered runner.
nomeatathlete.com

Travel, Socializing, and Dining Out

Happy Cow
Free online vegetarian restaurant guide.
happycow.net

MeetUp
Search for "vegetarian," "vegan," "animal welfare," "healthy eating," and more to find activities and new friends, whether you're at home or away.
meetup.com

Green Earth Travel
This organization has been organizing world travel for veg tourists for more than twenty years.
greenearthtravel.com

Veg Voyages
Vegan-friendly adventure tour packages in Asia.
vegvoyages.com

Online Recipes

Forks Over Knives
Recipes, meal planning, and information on maximizing the health benefits of a vegetarian diet.
forksoverknives.com

Oh She Glows
An award-winning veg recipe site by best-selling cookbook author Angela Liddon.
ohsheglows.com

Vegetarian Times
One of the largest compendia of lacto-ovo veg and vegan recipes online.
vegetariantimes.com/recipes

The Vegan Experience
Plant-based recipes and technique-focused articles from James Beard Award–winning chef and food writer J. Kenji López-Alt.
seriouseats.com/vegan-experience

Vegetarian Cookbooks

Afro-Vegan by Bryant Terry
Features fresh, affordable, and healthy recipes
honoring food traditions of the African diaspora:
Caribbean food, soul food, traditional African
dishes, and more.

**Decolonize Your Diet by Luz Calvo
and Catriona Rueda Esquibel**
Focuses on the traditional healthy foods of the
Mesoamerican peoples and puts an emphasis on
indigenous American ingredients.

Homemade Vegan Pantry by Miyoko Schinner
A total game-changer regarding substitutions for
meat, egg, and dairy products.

**How It All Vegan! by Tanya Barnard
and Sarah Kramer**
Full of realistic, wallet-friendly meals you can
throw together in a snap.

The Moosewood Cookbook by Mollie Katzen
One of the first vegetarian cookbooks to reach a

wide audience, full of adorable hand-written and
illustrated recipes for hearty and homey meals.

Plenty by **Yotam Ottolenghi**
A must-have for fans of vegetable-forward lacto-
ovo vegetarian Mediterranean recipes.

Silk Road Cooking by **Najmieh Batmanglij**
Highlights traditional veg dishes of the lands
spanning from Italy through the Levant and into
Central and East Asia.

Veganomicon by **Isa Chandra Moskowitz and
Terry Hope Romero**
Full of robust plant-based possibilities, with solid
how-tos for beginner cooks.

Vegetarian India by **Madhur Jaffrey**
Indispensable if you want to learn the basics of
the veg-friendly cuisines on the Subcontinent.

Vegetarian Cooking for Everyone
by **Deborah Madison**
Widely regarded as a classic, a James Beard
Award winner, and one of the best-selling lacto-
ovo vegetarian cookbooks of all time.

Non-Veg Cookbooks and Writers for Cooking Basics

How to Cook Everything Vegetarian
by Mark Bittman

Will teach you just that. The author's non-veg improvisation bible *Mark Bittman's Kitchen Matrix* is also well worth your time.

Every Grain of Rice by Fuchsia Dunlop

Full of some of the best tofu and vegetable sections I've ever encountered, plus crucial techniques from the Chinese peasant kitchen. Even the meat recipes have sidebars on how to make them vegetarian.

Essentials of Classic Italian Cooking
by Marcella Hazan

Precise and trenchant instruction for mastering the nuances of pasta; simple, seasonal vegetables; and hearty bean dishes.

Wild Fermentation by Sandor Ellix Katz
Recommended if you're looking to add tart and complex homemade flavors to food, boost digestibility, and enjoy the benefits of probiotics.

The Joy of Cooking by Irma S. Rombauer and Marion Rombauer Becker
Called "a fundamental resource for any American cook" by Julia Child.

Acknowledgments

Huge thanks to my friends whose tips and tricks—from rice to roll-cutting to rauschbier—have enhanced my cooking over the years. Special thanks to Team Humane League, Strong Hearts, the Tenney House diaspora, Philly Vegan Lady Gang, Chris (one of the best cooks I know, and a huge help with this process!), Carm, Josh, Lori, Kaecyy, Tiffany, Amy, and especially to my parents for putting up with a twelve-year-old who insisted that she wasn't ever going to put another animal in her mouth . . . and who came to the same conclusion twenty years later about what would go on their own plates. Thanks to the Quirk crew, who have all touched this book in one way or another, but especially to Jane, Molly, and Elizabeth! Shout-out to everyone who's ever come to a Vegetarians in Publishing dinner! Shout-out to Brett for opening his mind to a Quirk book with bacon substitutions in it. I hope you like them! Big love to Woodstock Farm Sanctuary for what they do and for being a great place for me to get away and clear my head after drafting this book.